W9-CXT-241

SCIENCE OF THE SUMMER OLYMPICS

EDGE BOOKS

THE SCIENCE BEHIND

SOCCER, VOLLEYBALL, CYCLING, AND OTHER POPULAR SPORTS

by Stephanie Watson

Consultant:

Mark Walsh

Associate Professor of Exercise Science

Miami University

Oxford, OH

WITHDRAWAL

Property of
FAUQUIER COUNTY PUBLIC LIBRARY
11 Winchester Street
Warrenton, VA 20186

CAPSTONE PRESS
a capstone imprint

1000524248

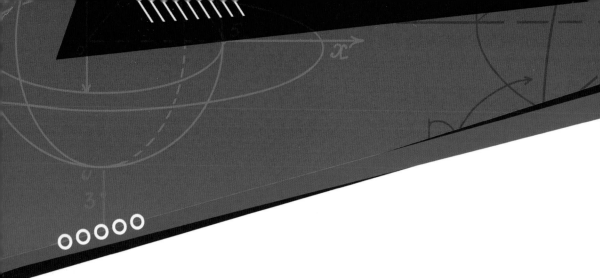

Edge Books are published by Capstone Press,
1710 Roe Crest Drive, North Mankato, Minnesota 56003
www.mycapstone.com

Copyright © 2016 by Capstone Press, a Capstone imprint. All rights reserved. No part of this publication may
be reproduced in whole or in part, or stored in a retrieval system, or transmitted in any form or by any means,
electronic, mechanical, photocopying, recording, or otherwise, without written permission of the publisher.

Library of Congress Cataloging-in-Publication Data
Names: Watson, Stephanie, 1969- author.
Title: The science behind soccer, volleyball, and other popular sports / by Stephanie Watson.
Other titles: Edge books. Science of the Summer Olympics.
Description: North Mankato, Minnesota : Capstone Press, a Capstone imprint, 2016. | ?2016 | Series: Edge
    books. Science of the Summer Olympics | Includes bibliographical references and index. | Audience: 8-9.? |
    Audience: 4 to 6.?
Identifiers: LCCN 2015035050| ISBN 9781491481608 (library binding) | ISBN 1491481609 (library binding) |
    ISBN 9781491481646 (pbk.) | ISBN 1491481641 (pbk.) | ISBN 9781491481684 (ebook pdf)
Subjects: LCSH: Sports--Juvenile literature. | Soccer—Juvenile literature. | Volleyball--Juvenile literature. |
    Sports sciences—Juvenile literature. | Olympics--Juvenile literature.
Classification: LCC GV705.4 .W45 2016 | DDC 796--dc23
LC record available at http://lccn.loc.gov/2015035050

Editorial Credits
Arnold Ringstad, editor
Craig Hinton, designer
Laura Polzin, production specialist

Photo Credits
AP Images: Alastair Grant, 4 (top), Andrew Matthews/Press Association, 16–17, Dave Thompson/Press
Association, 26, Dusan Vranic, 12, EMPICS Sport/Press Association, 1, 28 (background), Karl-Josef
Hildenbrand/picture-alliance/dpa, 10, Lefteris Pitarakis, 29 (left), Luca Bruno, cover, Mark Ralston, 13, Petr
David Josek, 11 (left), Rebecca Naden/Press Association, 21, Saurabh Das, 24, Scott Heppell, 11 (right),
Sergey Ponomarev, 28 (foreground), Tim Clarke/Express Newspapers, 29 (right), Vincent Thian, 6, Xiao Yong/
Imaginechina, 18; iStockphoto: majorosl, 8–9, Nastco, 20 (bottom), otisabi, 4 (bottom left), 4 (bottom right),
5 (left), 5 (right), ozgurdonmaz, 20 (top), simonkr, 14–15, Tivoly, 25; Dorling Kindersley/Thinkstock, 22–23

Printed in the United States of America in North Mankato, Minnesota
102015   2015CAP

TABLE OF CONTENTS

Chapter 1
Summer Olympics Science.................... 5

Chapter 2
Team Sports..................................... 7

Chapter 3
Net Sports.......................................19

Chapter 4
Cycling 27

Glossary 30
Read More... 31
**Critical Thinking
Using the Common Core** 31
Internet Sites 31
Index... 32

Cyclists race around the track during the 2004 Athens Olympics.

OLYMPIC COURTS AND FIELDS

Grass creates friction that slows a rolling or bouncing ball.

The hard wooden surface allows a basketball to bounce high.

soccer field

» approximately 328 feet (100 meters) long

» approximately 210 feet (64 m) wide

basketball court

» 92 feet (28 m) long

» 49 feet (15 m) wide

» Baskets: 10 feet (3 m) off the floor

CHAPTER 1

SUMMER OLYMPICS
SCIENCE

A cyclist maintains her balance around a sharp curve. A rugby sevens team smashes into its opponents with great force. A soccer player kicks the ball and watches it curve in midair into the goal.

Every Olympic sport requires skill and strength. But did you know that science also plays an important role in earning Olympic gold medals? From the bounce of a basketball to the spin of a bicycle wheel, scientific principles are at work. In some cases, athletes who know how to use biology and the laws of physics can gain an advantage over their opponents.

The height of the net makes it easier to hit shots over the center of the net, rather than the sides.

The height of the net means players must leap into the air to hit hard downward shots.

tennis court
» 78 feet (23.8 m) long
» 36 feet (11 m) wide
» Net: 3 feet, 6 inches (1.1 m) high at posts; 3 feet (0.9 m) high at center

volleyball court
» 59 feet (18 m) long
» 29 feet, 6 inches (9 m) wide
» Net: 8 feet (2.4 m) high for men; 7 feet, 4 inches (2.2 m) high for women

Italian player Giuseppe Rossi moves the ball away from a South Korean player during the 2008 Beijing Olympics.

CHAPTER 2

TEAM
SPORTS

In 1900 soccer became the first team sport in the Olympic games. The players are divided into two teams. They try to kick the ball into the other team's goal. Each team has a player called the goalkeeper who tries to protect its goal.

Every time a player kicks a motionless soccer ball, Sir Isaac Newton's first law of motion comes into play. The law says that an object at rest stays at rest and an object in motion stays in motion until an outside force interferes. In soccer the outside force is the player's foot. The soccer ball is at rest until a player kicks it. Then the force of the foot striking the ball puts it into motion. The ball keeps moving until the forces of **friction** and Earth's **gravity**—or other players—stop it.

friction—a force generated when objects slide past each other; the force also keeps motionless objects from sliding past each other
gravity—a force that causes objects to move toward Earth's center

Soccer Balls

Soccer balls are designed to bounce high and fly through the air. A soccer ball weighs 1 pound (0.45 kilograms). It's hollow and filled with high-pressure air. The outside of the ball is covered in a synthetic leather-like material, which is lighter than real leather. This helps the ball fly farther. A rubber bladder inside the ball holds the air. Layers of cotton or polyester form a lining between the cover and bladder. The lining helps the ball keep its shape and bounce.

friction

» When the ball drops to the ground, friction against the grass makes it slow down.

FORCES IN A SOCCER KICK

kicking force

» When a player kicks a soccer ball, the energy of his foot puts force on the ball. This force makes the ball fly up into the air and spin.

air resistance

» **Air resistance** makes the ball lose speed and forward momentum.

gravity

» Gravity causes the ball to drop to the ground.

During the kick, a player's foot touches the ball for about 0.01 seconds. As the ball rises into the air it starts to spin. This spinning motion makes the air on one side of the ball move faster than the air on the other side. The ball changes direction and curves—hopefully into the goal! This curve is known as the **Magnus effect**. Newton first described the effect in the 1670s.

air resistance—a force that acts against an object in motion, slowing it down
Magnus effect—a lift force that acts on a ball as it spins through the air; the Magnus effect makes a spinning ball curve in flight after it is kicked or hit

A type of friction called air resistance slows a ball in the air. The air molecules through which the ball passes slow it down. This force is known as **drag**. Another force is known as lift. It occurs when the air on one side of the ball moves faster than the air on the other side. The Magnus effect is one type of lift force. This can cause the ball to curve. Lift forces make the ball shift around and bounce in the air. Drag can make the ball hard to control in flight. The size, shape, and surface of the ball affect how much drag and lift occur. Drag, lack of control, and a good goalie make it hard for soccer players to score a lot of goals. On average, teams score fewer than three combined goals during each Olympic soccer match.

OLYMPIC SOCCER BALLS COMPARED

The soccer balls used in the Olympics have often featured advanced technology. These advances have sometimes led to changes in the way the ball has behaved on the field. Here are a few examples:

2004 Olympics: Pelias

» A new stitching technique results in smaller seams between panels, giving the ball more speed.

2008 Olympics: Magnus Moenia

» This ball's texture of tiny bumps gives it a faster spin rate.

2012 Olympics: The Albert

» A new bladder technology holds air inside the ball more effectively and prevents the ball from absorbing water, keeping it lightweight.

drag—the force that slows an object in motion traveling in air or water

HANG TIME
ooooo

Basketball players sometimes look like they're hanging in midair. This is called **"hang time."** As soon as a player jumps into the air, gravity begins pulling him back down. He starts to lose upward speed. At the top of his jump, his vertical speed reaches zero. Then his downward speed begins to increase. The player's lowest speed is at the top of the jump, so he spends more time there than in the lower parts of the jump.

Seventy-one percent of the time is spent in the top half of the jump height.

top half of jump

bottom half of jump

Twenty-nine percent of the time is spent in the bottom half of the jump height.

Australian player Lauren Jackson goes up for a shot against Canada's Tamara Tatham in the 2012 London Olympics.

Basketball

Basketball is played on a hard court. Two teams of five players dribble and pass the ball down the court. They score by throwing the ball into baskets at the ends of the court. The baskets are 10 feet (3 m) above the floor.

To move the ball down the court, the rules of basketball say that players must dribble it. They bounce the ball from their hands down to the floor and back up to their hands. As the ball leaves a player's hand, it has potential energy. This is the energy the ball has when it's in the air, thanks to gravity. As the ball drops, this potential energy converts to kinetic energy—the energy of motion.

hang time—the time when a basketball player hangs in the air during a jump

THE PERFECT
FREE THROW

Aim for a spot 2.8 inches (7.1 centimeters) back from the center of the hoop.

In 2008, engineering professor Larry Silverberg at North Carolina State University studied millions of possible basketball shots. He found the formula for the perfect free throw for a typical player based on the distance from the hoop and the force of gravity.

When the ball hits the floor, some of this energy is lost. A small amount of the energy is lost by flattening the bottom of the ball slightly, causing the temperature of the ball to increase a tiny bit. But most of the energy goes down into the floor and back up into the ball, causing the ball to bounce up to the dribbler's hand. To keep the ball moving down the court, players must keep putting energy into it by dribbling over and over.

When players shoot, their fingertips make the ball spin backward. This is called backspin. When a ball with backspin hits the backboard, its horizontal velocity slows and it bounces back and downward toward the net. The backspin makes it more likely to go in.

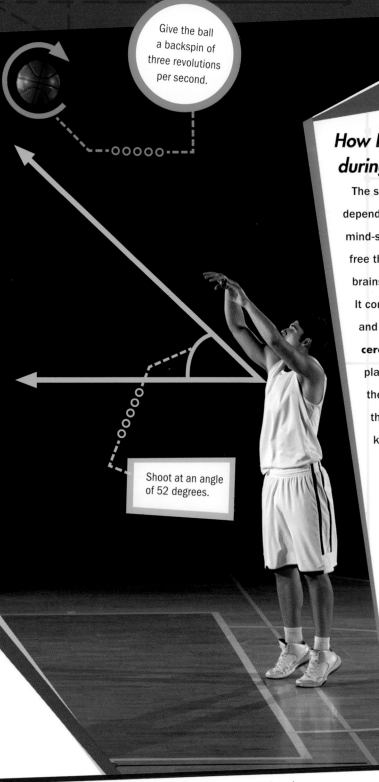

Give the ball a backspin of three revolutions per second.

Shoot at an angle of 52 degrees.

How Does the Brain Work during a Free Throw?

The success of a free throw can depend on the player's brain and mind-set. To learn how to shoot a free throw, players use a part of their brains called the **cerebral cortex**. It controls thought. As they practice and get good at the shot, the **cerebellum** takes over. It gives players the fast motor skills they need to throw the shot into the basket. This is sometimes known as muscle memory.

During the game a player might concentrate hard on hitting the free throw. Thinking hard activates the cerebral cortex again. This part of the brain isn't very good at working fast under pressure. That's why some players "choke" in big games, such as the Olympic gold-medal game, and miss the free throw.

cerebral cortex—the part of the brain that controls thought
cerebellum—the part of the brain that controls muscles and movement

15

Rugby

Rugby was last in the Olympics in 1924. In the 2016 Summer Olympics, a type of rugby called rugby sevens will be a part of the Olympics for the first time. In rugby sevens, each team has seven players instead of the usual 15 players. Rugby sevens is faster-paced than regular rugby.

Teams try to carry or pass the ball past a goal line at each end of the field to score. Play often begins with a scrum. Members of each team crouch down across from each other. They lock arms and lunge at each other. The ball is thrown into the gap between the front rows of players. Players try to kick the ball back toward teammates with their feet. The team that gets the ball runs it down the field.

The size and strength of rugby players lead to massive forces during a scrum.

During a scrum Newton's second law of motion comes into play. The law states that force is equal to mass multiplied by acceleration. The mass in this equation is the combined mass of all the players. The acceleration is a measure of how quickly they go from standing still to smashing into one another. One scrum can generate up to 1.5 tons (1.4 metric tons) of force. That's almost as powerful as the bite of a great white shark!

U.S. player Heather Bown spikes the ball during a match against China in the 2008 Beijing Olympics.

CHAPTER 3

NET **SPORTS**

In volleyball, the goal is to score points by keeping the ball in the air. If the ball hits the ground on a team's side, the other team scores a point.

The server throws the ball into the air and then hits it with her palm to make it fall on the other side of the net. The two teams battle to keep sending the ball back and forth. Hitting at a downward angle with a lot of force makes the ball hard for the other team to return. This is called a **spike**. Bulgarian men's Olympic volleyball player Matey Kaziyski once spiked a volleyball at 82 miles (132 kilometers) per hour!

A basic knowledge of psychology, the science of thinking and behavior, can give alert volleyball players an advantage. The way an opponent stands or bends an elbow can give clues about where she will move next or how she will hit the ball. Sometimes looks can be deceiving, though. A player might lean one way and then dive the other way to fake out the other team.

spike—hitting the volleyball to make it fly over the net at a downward angle

Tennis

Tennis was part of the 1896 Games in Athens, Greece. This was the first modern Olympics. The sport is played on a rectangular court divided by a net in the middle. In singles tennis, one player is on either side of the net. Doubles tennis has two teams of two players each.

TENNIS RACKETS
YESTERDAY AND TODAY

For many years, tennis rackets were made from wood. They had a long handle and a small head. Modern rackets are made from graphite mixed with titanium, Kevlar, or other fibers. These materials are strong but much lighter than wood. Lighter rackets are easier to swing and help players hit the ball faster. The larger surface area of modern rackets also gives today's players finer control over the spin on the ball.

New racket
» Frame material: composite, including graphite and other strong, light materials
» String material: nylon
» Weight: 7–13 ounces (200–370 grams)

Old racket
» Frame material: wood
» String material: animal intestine
» Weight: 13–15 ounces (370–425 g)

British player Andy Murray won the gold medal in men's singles tennis at the 2012 London Olympic Games.

Players hit the ball across the net. They score a point if their opponent can't hit the ball back or if the opponent hits it out of bounds.

The ball enters play in the serve. During the serve the player rotates his legs, hips, trunk, and shoulders to build energy. He tosses the ball into the air. Then he transfers the energy from his body to his arm. He swings his arm down and flicks his wrist to put **topspin** on the ball. Thanks to the Magnus effect, a ball with topspin falls quickly to the court on the other side of the net. This helps the ball land in bounds. Some types of serves use other styles of spin.

topspin—the forward spin on a ball around its center; this forces the ball to fall sooner than usual, making it harder for the opponent to return

TRACKING
THE BALL

ooooo

With players serving at speeds well over 100 miles (161 km) per hour, it can be difficult to be certain about whether a serve lands in or out of bounds. A system called Hawk-Eye has changed this. The system is made up of several video cameras that record the ball's movement from different angles. The cameras feed this data to a central computer, which builds a three-dimensional model of the ball's path through the air. The system is accurate to within 0.2 inches (5 millimeters).

The Science behind the Grunt

A highlight of the 2012 Summer Olympics was a match between Serena Williams and Maria Sharapova. Both players are known for making loud grunting noises when they hit the ball. Sharapova's grunts can reach 93 decibels—as loud as a jackhammer!

Grunting sounds funny, but it can help. When players grunt they tighten their stomach muscles and breathe out. This gives them more power to swing the racket. One study found grunting increased serve speeds by 5 miles (8 km) per hour.

Rafael Nadal is a Spanish tennis player who won a gold medal in the 2008 Beijing Olympics. His serve spins at about 60 revolutions per second. It rotates about 80 times from when he hits it until it drops on the other side of the court.

Tennis matches can be played on hard, clay, or grass courts. The surface changes how the ball bounces. Most Olympic matches are played on hard courts made from concrete. Balls hit the surface and bounce back up at a faster speed than on courts made of softer materials. Clay courts are made from packed clay or sand. They are softer, so the ball bounces higher and slower. The surfaces absorb more of the ball's energy. Grass courts can be difficult to play on. The ball sometimes bounces unevenly on the bumpy ground.

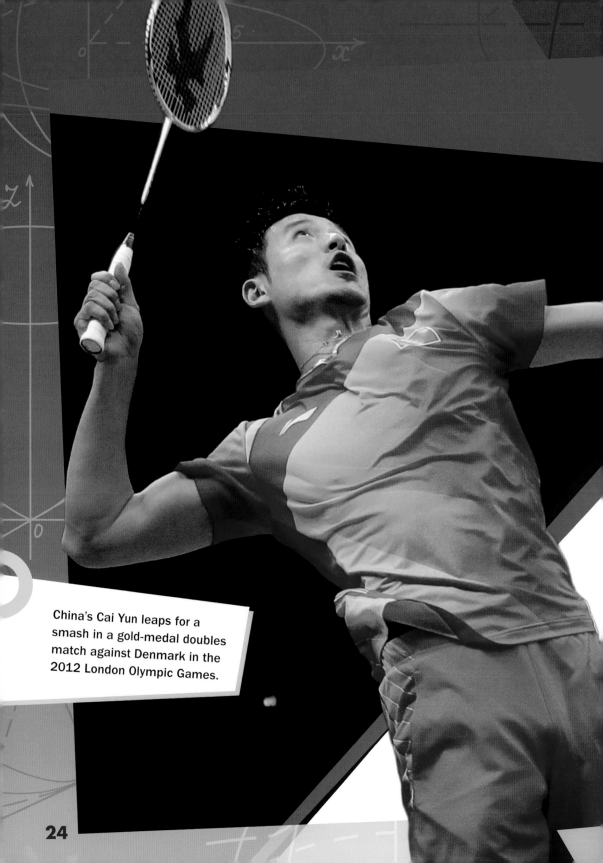

China's Cai Yun leaps for a smash in a gold-medal doubles match against Denmark in the 2012 London Olympic Games.

Badminton

Of all the Olympic sports, badminton may be the fastest. Players use rackets to keep a shuttlecock in the air. They can hit the shuttlecock over the net at speeds of more than 160 miles (257 km) per hour.

The shuttlecock is a small piece of cork with feathers attached to it. The feathers are taken from the left wing of a goose so the shuttlecock spins clockwise. Feathers from the right wing would spin it the opposite way. When the players hit the shuttlecock, it quickly accelerates to a high speed. As it flies through the air, the feathers cause high drag and slow it.

The average badminton **rally** is only about seven seconds long. Players have to react quickly. As they lunge and jump, their hearts pound to send additional blood to their muscles.

rally—an exchange of shots in tennis, volleyball, badminton, and other net sports

Marianne Vos of the Netherlands wins a road race in the 2012 London Olympic Games.

CHAPTER 4

CYCLING

The Summer Olympics includes four types of cycling: road race, track, BMX, and mountain biking. The road race is held on an open road. Races are long, and riders need a lot of stamina. The 2012 Olympic cycling road race took riders all over London, England.

Track cycling is held on an oval racetrack called a **velodrome**. At each end is a curve with a 42-degree angle. The angle creates **centripetal force**. It pushes cyclists toward the curved turn so they can ride fast without sliding off the edge of the track. Track cyclists can reach speeds of more than 50 miles (80 km) per hour.

BMX is short for bicycle motocross. Eight riders compete on a dirt track. They navigate jumps, obstacles, and tight turns. Mountain biking is done off-road. Bikers power their way over uneven ground. They go up and down hills and ride through forests. Both BMX and mountain bikers need speed and strength to traverse the rough courses.

velodrome—a steeply curved, oval-shaped cycling track
centripetal force—a force that acts on a cyclist who is moving in a circle; centripetal force pushes a track cyclist toward the center of the curve and keeps her on the track

When a cyclist turns the pedals of a bike with his feet, the kinetic energy generated by his muscles makes the bike speed up. A few forces work against a cyclist to slow him. When he rides uphill, he has to work against the force of gravity. As he speeds up, air resistance pushes against his bike and body.

A road cyclist can lower drag by staying close to the rider in front of him. The cyclist in front creates a pocket of air called a slipstream. This pocket shields the second rider from air resistance.

OLYMPIC BICYCLES

Olympic bikes are designed differently for each type of race:

BMX bike

Mountain and BMX bikes have small, wide wheels. The wider surface area lets the wheels grip rough terrain. Air pressure is lower than in track bikes, helping absorb impacts from bumpy ground.

mountain bike

Track and road bikes are made from carbon fiber. They're light but strong. Their tires are narrow and smooth to increase speed. They are filled with high-pressure air to reduce friction against the track. This lets the bikes go faster.

road bike

track bike

Helmets are designed to make road cyclists go fast. An **aerodynamic** helmet can shave one minute off every 25-mile (40-km) race compared to a normal bicycle helmet. Racers wear a teardrop-shaped helmet with a long tail to help the helmet slip smoothly through the air and reduce drag. The helmet has very few air vents. Vents cause air to bounce around a rider's head, slowing her down.

Using Science to Win Gold

Athletes in a wide variety of popular Olympic sports use science to get an edge on their opponents. They use natural forces, such as drag, friction, gravity, and lift, to their advantage. They serve tennis balls and shoot free throws at precise angles. They put their minds to work using psychology and muscle memory. In the modern Olympics, the athletes who use science to their advantage have a better chance at going home with a gold medal.

aerodynamic—a shape that reduces the amount of drag on an object; being aerodynamic increases speed

GLOSSARY

aerodynamic (air-oh-dye-NAM-mik)—a shape that reduces the amount of drag on an object; being aerodynamic increases speed

air resistance (AIR ri-ZISS-tuhnss)—a force that acts against an object in motion, slowing it down

centripetal force (sen-TRI-puh-tul FORSS)—a force that acts on a cyclist who is moving in a circle; centripetal force pushes a track cyclist toward the center of the curve and keeps her on the track

cerebellum (sayr-uh-BELL-um)—the part of the brain that controls muscles and movement

cerebral cortex (suh-REEB-ruhl COR-tex)—the part of the brain that controls thought

drag (DRAG)—the force that slows an object in motion traveling in air or water

friction (FRIK-shuhn)—a force generated when objects slide past each other; the force also keeps motionless objects from sliding past each other

gravity (GRAV-uh-tee)—a force that causes objects to move toward Earth's center

hang time (HANG time)—the time when a basketball player hangs in the air during a jump

Magnus effect (MAG-nus uh-FEKT)—a lift force that acts on a ball as it spins through the air; the Magnus effect makes a spinning ball curve in flight after it is kicked or hit

rally (RAL-ee)—an exchange of shots in tennis, volleyball, badminton, and other net sports

spike (SPIKE)—hitting the volleyball to make it fly over the net at a downward angle

topspin (TOP-spin)—the forward spin on a ball around its center; this forces the ball to fall sooner than usual, making it harder for the opponent to return

velodrome (VELL-oh-drome)—a steeply curved, oval-shaped cycling track

READ MORE

Graubart, Norman D. *The Science of Basketball.* Sports Science.
New York: PowerKids Press, 2015.

Herman, Gail. *What Are the Summer Olympics?* What Was . . . ?
New York: Grosset & Dunlap, 2016.

CRITICAL THINKING USING THE COMMON CORE

1. Look at the diagrams of Olympic courts and fields on pages
4 and 5. Based on these images and the measurements listed,
which sports involve the most running? Which involve the most
jumping? How might long-term endurance and short-term quickness
play a role in each sport? (Integration of Knowledge and Ideas)

2. This book describes how spin on the ball is a factor in soccer,
basketball, and tennis. How does the use of spin differ in each
sport? How do athletes use this spin to their advantages? Support
your answers with at least two other print or online sources.
(Integration of Knowledge and Ideas)

INTERNET SITES

FactHound offers a safe, fun way to find Internet sites related to
this book. All of the sites on FactHound have been researched by
our staff.

Visit *www.facthound.com*

Type in this code: 9781491481608

Check out projects, games and lots more at
www.capstonekids.com

INDEX

air resistance, 9, 10, 28

badminton, 25
basketball, 4, 12–15

cycling
    BMX, 27, 28
    mountain, 27, 28
    road race, 27, 28–29
    track, 27, 29

drag, 10, 25, 28, 29

free throws, 14–15
friction, 7, 8, 10, 29

gravity, 7, 12, 13, 28, 29

hang time, 12
Hawk-Eye system, 22
helmets, 29

Kaziyski, Matey, 19

Magnus effect, 9, 10, 21

Nadal, Rafael, 23
Newton, Sir Isaac, 7, 9, 17

psychology, 19, 29

rackets, 20, 22, 25
rugby sevens, 5, 16–17

scrum, 16–17
serves, 19, 21, 22, 23, 29
Sharapova, Maria, 22
shuttlecock, 25
soccer, 4, 7–11
spikes, 19
spin, 9, 11, 14, 15, 20, 21, 23, 25

tennis, 5, 20–23

velodrome, 27
volleyball, 5, 19

Williams, Serena, 22